WORLD'S MOST
ENDANGERED

—

By Karen McGhee

Australian
GEOGRAPHIC

WORLD'S MOST
ENDANGERED

World's Most Endangered is published by Australian Geographic, an imprint of Bauer Media Ltd. All images and text are copyright © Bauer Media and may not be reproduced without the written permission of the publishers.

First published in 2015 by:

MEDIA GROUP

Bauer Media
54 Park Street, Sydney, NSW 2000
Telephone: (02) 9263 9813
Fax: (02) 9216 3731
Email: editorial@ausgeo.com.au

www.australiangeographic.com.au

Australian Geographic customer service:
1300 555 176 (local call rate within Australia).
From overseas +61 2 8667 5295

Editor Lauren Smith
Text Karen McGhee
Book design Mike Ellott
Picture research Jess Teideman
Print production Chris Clear
Sub-editor Carolyn Barry and Natsumi Penberthy
Proof reader Ken Eastwood
Managing Director Matthew Stanton
Publishing Director – Specialist Division Brendon Hill
Publisher Jo Runciman
Editor-in-Chief, Australian Geographic Chrissie Goldrick

Printed in China by C & C Offset Printing Co. Ltd.

RELATED TITLES:

WORLD'S MOST
ENDANGERED

Earth is facing an extinction crisis. By the middle of this century, it's thought that half of the animals and plants that currently share our planet could be gone forever. The animals in this book are among those we're most likely to lose, unless we can help them.

CONTENTS

BY THE NUMBERS

The International Union for Conservation of Nature (IUCN) has assessed over 46,000 different animal species. Its job is to determine the status of each animal species, identifying those animals that are of least concern, and drawing attention to those that are on the path to extinction. It's not a pretty picture.

IUCN RED LIST CATEGORY

Least Concern

Near Threatened

Vulnerable

Endangered

Critically Endangered

Extinct In The Wild

Extinct

25,283

1884 animal species have been defined as 'critically endangered', meaning they face an extremely high risk of extinction in the wild. All of the animals in this book are critically endangered.

AMPHIBIANS
525

BIRDS
213

MAMMALS
213

FISHES
423

REPTILES
168

ARTHROPODS
342

There are hundreds of 'critically endangered' species that are actually thought to be extinct. Until they can confirm that, they don't change the status – but the true number of extinctions is likely much higher.

2760 4478 3114 1884 18 418

ASIA
AMUR LEOPARD

GREATEST THREAT

HABITAT LOSS

GREATEST THREAT

HUNTING

Fewer than 35 Amur leopards survive in the wild, making this one of the world's most endangered big cats. Its usual habitat is forests in north-eastern China and south-eastern Russia, though it's now thought to be extinct in China. Because the Amur is prized for its stunning, luxurious coat and its bones are used in Chinese medicine, poachers have been a major threat.

FACT BOX — NICE AND NIMBLE

This rare leopard is perfectly adapted to hunt small deer and hares. It is fast and agile, able to run at speeds of almost 60km/h and make leaps 6m long and 3m high.

GREATEST THREAT HUNTING

◀ SAIGA

Between the early 1990s and 2005, the saiga population crashed by more than 95 per cent from one million to a few thousand. This was mostly because of hunting for their meat and the horns of the males. Overgrazing of their pastures (dry grasslands and semi-desert areas) by introduced livestock, particularly sheep, has also played a big role.

FACT BOX **Ice Age survivor**

This strange-looking nomadic herd animal, part way between a sheep and an antelope, is a relict of the last Ice Age when sabre-toothed tigers and woolly mammoths roamed the Earth.

SUMATRAN ORANGUTAN

Found only on the Indonesian island of Sumatra, this is the rarer of the two orangutan species. Only 6600 Sumatran orangutans now survive in the wild, mainly because of **habitat** destruction. The tropical forests the species calls home are being logged, mostly to make way for palm oil plantations. If this continues at current rates, the Sumatran orangutan is likely to be extinct in the wild within 50 years.

WILD COUSINS

Orangutans are actually close relatives of humans. They have a similar life span and, like us, mother orangutans are pregnant for nine months.

SUMATRAN AND SOUTH CHINA TIGERS

A century ago there were eight tiger subspecies and about 100,000 tigers roamed Asia. Three subspecies are extinct, and the South China tiger is considered 'functionally extinct' because it hasn't been seen in the wild for 25 years. Fewer than 400 wild Sumatran tigers survive. Tigers are now protected and trade in their body parts is illegal. But poaching, particularly for **Chinese medicine**, continues to have a huge impact.

MEDICAL EXTINCTION

There's a Chinese medicine market for almost every part of the tiger's body: eyeballs are an epilepsy treatment; whiskers a toothache remedy.

SUMATRAN ELEPHANT

This elephant became recognised as one of world's most endangered animals in 2011 after half of its population disappeared in just 25 years. Almost three-quarters of its habitat was destroyed over that time. The only place it survives in the wild is Sumatra, which has one of the world's highest **deforestation** rates. Because of that, the elephants are forced into contact with villages where they're killed when they raid crops, trample homes or threaten people.

IVORY TARGETS

Only male Sumatran elephants have tusks. They're smaller than those of other elephants, but still seen by poachers as a valuable source of ivory

ASIA

PEACOCK TARANTULA

So far, the only place this tarantula has ever been found in the wild is a small patch of land, less than 100sq.km in size, on the eastern coast of India. A large spider with a leg span of about 20cm, it lives in deep crevices on old trees. Although the home range of the spider is protected within a state forest reserve, people from nearby villages cut down trees in the reserve for firewood and timber.

FACT BOX   Spider pet

This tarantula's name comes from its stunning and rare blue colouration, which makes it popular with spider collectors worldwide.

PAINTED BATAGUR

Overexploitation has been a major reason this Asian turtle has become so endangered. People catch and eat the adults and raid their nests to harvest the eggs for food. Trading the eggs is now illegal, but on the **black market** they can fetch more than 25 times the value of chicken eggs. The species is also popular worldwide in the pet trade because of the striking appearance of the males, which change colour during the breeding season.

GREATEST THREAT
HABITAT LOSS

GREATEST THREAT
HUNTING

MATING MOVES

Adults live in freshwater in rivers in Malaysia, Sumatra, Borneo and Thailand, but migrate downstream to lay eggs in mangroves and beach nests.

The bulbous tip on the male's snout is thought to be involved in attracting females.

GREATEST THREAT
HABITAT LOSS

FACT BOX

Huge but harmless

Male gharials can grow longer than 6m. Although their long narrow snout is studded with razor sharp teeth, they use it for attacking fish and it's not suited for chomping anything the size of a person.

FIGHTING BACK

Poaching is illegal hunting. It's the biggest threat to many animal species around the world, including elephants, tigers and rhinos. Animals are poached because they have body parts that are considered highly valuable. Countries are now getting very tough with poachers. In parts of Africa and China, for example, poaching can be punished with fines and long jail sentences. And wildlife rangers are being trained to shoot poachers who resist arrest.

◄ GHARIAL

Captive breeding has been helping this crocodile species since the 1980s. Eggs collected in the wild are hatched in captivity and young crocodiles released back into their natural habitat. Unfortunately, human settlements have been growing rapidly in the areas they inhabit and so it's hard to find release sites where they'll be safe.

ASIA

SUNDA PANGOLIN

A large illegal international trade in pangolins and their body parts threatens this mammal's survival. Their meat is eaten as a delicacy. Their scales, which are made of a hardened hair-like material and cover and protect their bodies, are ground up as a medicine, and their hide is used to make shoes. Sunda pangolins were once common in forests, grasslands and even plantations across much of Southeast Asia – from Vietnam, Cambodia and Thailand to Malaysia, Singapore and Indonesia. Most populations however, have now crashed.

GREATEST THREAT HUNTING

Pangolins eat almost nothing but ants and termites and a single adult is thought to eat about 70 million of these insects in a year.

SIAU ISLAND TARSIER

These tiny **primates** have always had it tough. They live on only one small Indonesian island called Siau, which is dominated by one of the world's most active volcanoes, Mt Karangetang. Despite that, tarsiers are thought to have survived there for millions of years. Now, the island's human population has been expanding and altered most of the tarsier's habitat. Beyond that, the local people are catching and eating the tarsier.

Scientists only discovered the Siau Island tarsier in 2005 and already it faces a high risk of extinction.

CHINESE GIANT SALAMANDER

This massive nocturnal creature is thought to be capable of growing to a length of about 1.8m, making it the world's largest amphibian. But now the species is so rare that specimens longer than about 1m are hardly ever seen. Its biggest threat is over-harvesting. People hunt and capture giant salamanders because they're regarded as a luxury food. Their body parts are also in demand for traditional medicines.

RESERVATION RESCUES

At least six nature reserves have been set up in China to protect giant salamanders and their habitat.

GREATEST THREAT

HABITAT LOSS

PHILIPPINE EAGLE

The numbers in the wild of this bird of prey have probably always been low, because it's a carnivore at the top of its food chain. But now that most of their mountain forest habitat has been destroyed, fewer than 500 survive. Poisonous pesticides in the environment may also be having an impact by reducing the number of eggs that hatch.

FACT BOX — Longest eagle

Females are thought to grow bigger than males and can grow to more than a metre from bill to tail – longer than any other eagle.

GREATEST
THREAT

HABITAT LOSS

IBERIAN
LYNX

Could this be the first cat species to become extinct in 2000 years? In 2007, it certainly looked like that was likely to happen when it was estimated that there were as few as 100 Iberian lynx surviving in the wild. That included just 25 females capable of breeding. Since then, fortunately, numbers have increased slightly due partly to the release of animals from captive breeding programs. However, the Iberian lynx remains the world's rarest cat species. One reason has been the decline of its main prey, rabbits, through over-hunting and disease.

FACT BOX — Dwindling distribution

The Iberian lynx was once found across Spain, Portugal and parts of France. Now there are only two very small breeding populations, both in southern Spain.

GREATEST THREAT HUNTING

NORTH ATLANTIC RIGHT WHALE

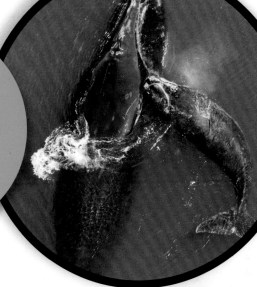

Commercial whaling of the North Atlantic right whale was banned in 1935 and it has been protected ever since. Many were killed before then though, and the species struggled to recover. This is mostly because these animals live a long time, up to 70 years, and reproduce slowly. Once, the species was common on both sides of the Atlantic. Now as few as 300 survive on the western side, and it's thought to be extinct on the eastern side.

Did you know?

This species was given its common name because it was considered the 'right' species for whalers to target.

MEDITERRANEAN MONK SEAL

Many thousands of Mediterranean monk seals once lived along the coastlines of Europe and northwest Africa. After centuries of human disturbance in these areas, fewer than 500 are thought to survive. Commercial fishing is now one of the biggest threats to the species' survival, as the seals become tangled and drown in fishing gear. Also, they're killed by fishermen who think they compete for fish. Education campaigns for fisherman are underway to try and reduce their impact on the remaining seals.

BATUECAN ROCK LIZARD

This is the rarest reptile in mainland Europe. There is just one known population, in Spain's Sierra de Francia mountain range. It contains between 100 and 250 adult lizards.

The species is threatened by impacts on its habitat from road construction. Tourist activity is also a problem. Reptile collectors, attracted by the lizard's rarity, are another threat.

NEW IDENTITY

The Batuecan rock lizard has only been confirmed as a separate species since 2003 and scientists know very little about it.

Scientists are developing captive breeding programs to help save the European mink.

GREATEST THREAT
HUNTING

EUROPEAN MINK

This mammal was a famed source of fur for the fashion industry last century. Over-hunting for fur has seriously reduced its numbers. But that is just one in a series of threats that has brought this species close to extinction. The mink is semi-aquatic and it needs a clean river habitat to survive. Many of the waterways where it lives have been degraded by development and pollution. In the 1920s the American mink was introduced and that has also taken its toll. The larger American species took over the food and territory of its European cousin.

LADIES' FUR NECKWEAR

AEOLIAN WALL LIZARD

This lizard is found only in four small isolated populations in the Aeolian Islands, northeast of Sicily. It is feared that a disease or disaster could wipe out one of these populations, bringing the species close to extinction. The largest population is also thought to suffer from competition by the Italian wall lizard, an introduced species.

POSSIBLE ANSWERS

Captive breeding is one of the strategies being considered to ensure the survival of the Aeolian wall lizard. Introducing this species to other islands in the Aeolian chain might also give the species a better chance at survival.

DESERTAS WOLF SPIDER

A weed is thought to be behind a fall in numbers of the Desertas wolf spider. The only place in the world where this rare arachnid is known to occur is a valley on the north side of the Deserta Grande Island, off the north-west coast of Africa. Invasion by the introduced plant known as bulbous canarygrass has changed the ecosystem in the valley and altered the spider's habitat. It's meant that the area in which the spider is known to occur has been reduced by about three-quarters.

FACT BOX

Chemical solution

One solution for this rare spider species might be spraying herbicides to eradicate the weed that has altered its habitat.

KARPATHOS FROG

One river on the Greek island of Karpathos is the only known place where this frog lives. There are reports from the 1960s that the species was abundant, but it's been difficult to find since the early 1990s. The species seems to rely on clean water sources that are either still or slow-running. Like many frogs, it's likely to be very sensitive, and there may have been disturbances to its habitat that could be responsible for its decline.

GREATEST THREAT

HABITAT LOSS

The survival of the Karpathos frog at the one location where it's still known to occur might be due to the isolation of the island.

AFRICA
BLACK RHINO

GREATEST THREAT HUNTING

The single biggest threat to the black rhino is poaching. This illegal hunting is driven by a demand in Asia for rhino horns. These are ground up and used in Chinese medicine for a variety of ailments. However, rhino horns are made of keratin, the same protein as our own fingernails and hair and there is no proof they work as a medicine against any disease or disorder. Rhino horns are also valued by illegal buyers as symbols of wealth and success.

LEMURS

Lemurs are facing an extreme threat of extinction. There are 103 different species of these primates and 24 of them are now on the world's most endangered list. Lemurs are found only on the Indian Ocean island of Madagascar, which is located off the east coast of Africa. Though they are hunted for food, the main reason why so many are at risk of **extinction** is habitat destruction. Their tropical forest homes are being logged for timber and cleared for agriculture. About 90 per cent of Madagascar's vegetation has been altered or destroyed.

GREATEST THREAT

HABITAT LOSS

Turning lemurs into Madagascar's number one tourist attraction is being seen as a key way to help save this group of animals.

GREATEST THREAT

HABITAT LOSS

TARZAN CHAMELEON

There are many cases of animals facing extinction before we've had a chance to learn much about them and this is one! It was discovered in 2009 and identified as one of the world's most endangered animals just three years later. It is found only in Madagascar and, so far, is known only from two very small patches of forest. Both of them are in a degraded state, but there are efforts underway to protect what's left of this habitat.

LOWLAND GORILLA

Sadly, this is another species that's on the list because of illegal hunting. They're killed for food; their flesh is known as 'bushmeat'. Some of their body parts are used as medicines, or young gorillas can be captured to become pets. Another major risk faced by the species is disease, and on top of that, their habitat in Africa is being destroyed at a very fast rate. Their forests are being logged for timber and cleared for agriculture or new settlements.

DISEASE RISK

Since the early 1990s, Ebola has caused waves of death in gorilla and chimpanzee populations in Africa. The virus kills more than 95 per cent of infected gorillas.

GREATEST THREAT

HUNTING

AFRICA
MANTELLAS

GREATEST THREAT

HABITAT LOSS

Mantellas are tiny, bright frogs. They're another animal group that's found only on the island of Madagascar. At least three species are at risk of extinction and each occurs in a very limited area and in habitat that is mostly degraded. Mantellas have skin toxins that they absorb from the ants, termites and other insects they prey upon. It's a form of defence that makes these frogs distasteful and often poisonous to predators. But in some areas, where pollution and human development has caused declines in their prey, mantellas are becoming less toxic, which can make them tastier to predators.

FACT BOX

TOO POPULAR

Before habitat destruction became their biggest threat, overcollection caused huge falls in their numbers. They're in demand by enthusiasts the world over.

SPIDER TORTOISE & KLEINMANN'S TORTOISE

These two species, like turtles and tortoises all over the world, suffer from **overexploitation**. People eat their meat and their eggs, as well as collect them as pets. Many turtles are also sensitive to change and can't cope when their habitats become degraded. Development has already destroyed over half of the habitat of the spider tortoise, which is found only on Madagascar. Kleinmann's tortoise lives in desert and semi-desert habitats. It's also known as the Egyptian tortoise, however it is thought to be extinct in Egypt.

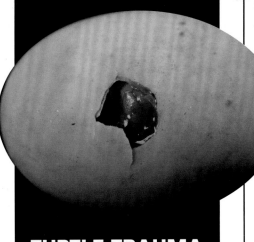

SPIDER TORTOISE

KLEINMANN'S TORTOISE

TURTLE TRAUMA

There are 320 species of turtle and tortoise in the world that live on land or in freshwater. After surviving for more than 200 million years, 57 species (nearly a fifth of the group) are now on the world's most endangered list.

COELACANTH

Once known only from fossils, this fish was thought to have died out over 60 million years ago. But it was found in 1938 around the Comoros islands, off Africa's east coast. Coelacanths live more than 100m down in the ocean and don't survive being brought to the surface. This rare fish is unlike any other living species, and is thought to be a link to the first animals that walked on land.

VOLUNTARY PROTECTION

Many Comoros island fishermen make sure they avoid catching coelacanths by keeping away from areas they're known to occur.

ADDAX

Addaxes once migrated across northern Africa in herds that could contain thousands of animals. Now, there are fewer than 300 individuals in the wild and they are only ever seen in groups of three or four. Local people have been hunting addaxes for centuries, but they became particularly good at it during the 20th century with the invention of technologies such as high-powered rifles.

BREEDING SUCCESSES

More addaxes live in zoos and collections than in the wild. About 600 are in breeding programs, and addaxes raised in captivity are starting to be released into protected reserves.

GREATEST THREAT HUNTING

CORROBOREE FROG

This Australian alpine frog species is another of the world's mountain-dwelling amphibians that has been mysteriously and rapidly disappearing during the past decade. Exotic trees, including willows, have invaded their habitat, which is also disturbed by feral pigs. And one summer, huge areas were destroyed by bushfires. But there's no single explanation for the huge losses of this stunning amphibian.

A captive breeding program is underway in zoos in an attempt to keep this frog from extinction. It's hoped that releasing tadpoles into streams will help the species survive.

GREATEST THREAT DISEASE

WOYLIE

Woylies once lived right across the bottom third of Australia. Now they're extinct in the east side of the country. And only a few small and isolated populations are left elsewhere, mostly in the southwest of the continent. Woylies, also known as brush-tailed bettongs, which look like small kangaroos, are marsupials. Their numbers crashed during the 20th century because of hunting by introduced predators, mainly foxes and cats.

MYSTERY DISAPPEARANCE

Conservation efforts from the 1970s managed to increase woylie numbers. But since 2001, the total population dropped again and no one is sure why.

GILBERT'S POTOROO

By the beginning of this century Gilbert's potoroo had become one of the world's rarest mammals. Only 30 individuals survived in one isolated population in a nature reserve in Western Australia. There was real concern that it would take just one natural disaster, like a fire, for the species to disappear forever. Since then, two new populations have been set up that are both protected from the feral predators that put the species on the world's most endangered list.

GOOD NEWS

The Gilbert's potoroo population has grown to almost 10 times the size it was in 2000. There are now more than 200 surviving in the wild.

EXTINCTION SHAME

In the past 200 years, 22 Australian mammals have become extinct. That's about 10% of Australia's mammal species and one-third of all mammals that have gone extinct worldwide during that time. It's one of the worst extinction rates for any country. The main cause has been feral animals. These introduced pests hunt native species, compete for their food and shelter, destroy habitat and spread disease. Australia's worst introduced predators have been foxes, cats and toads. Rabbits and camels are responsible for a lot of habitat damage.

MOUNTAIN PYGMY-POSSUM

The mountain pygmy-possum's most important source of food, the Bogong moth, is declining due to pesticide use. These moths usually swarm to the mountains for summer.

GREATEST THREAT

HABITAT LOSS

This little possum lives at high altitude and loves cold weather. It's the only mammal that lives exclusively in the Australian Alps and nowhere else. It manages this by being the only marsupial that hibernates. The mountain pygmy-possum now survives in just three separate small populations. Its habitat has suffered from the growth of Australia's ski industry and the development that's come with that. The possum is also struggling to cope with climate change. Already temperatures are increasing in the Alps and snow cover is decreasing. Feral predators, mostly foxes and cats, are another problem.

KAKAPO

It may be flightless, but the kakapo uses its wings! The wings help maintain balance while the kakapo is running or climbing; and also slow it down when it leaps from low trees.

As well as being one of the world's rarest birds, this parrot is unique in many ways. It is flightless and nocturnal, and the world's heaviest parrot, with adults reaching a weight of 3.5kg. The kakapo once lived across most of New Zealand, but it's been disappearing since human colonisation began there about 800 years ago. Kakapos have no defences against predators, and introduced species such as dogs, cats, rats and stoats have played a huge role in reducing their numbers.

FACT BOX

Tragic losses

The kakapo is now extinct from almost all the areas it once occurred. In 2012 just 126 were left.

BAW BAW FROG

A mid-1980s survey found more than 10,000 Baw Baw frogs in the wild. Just 10 years later this frog's population had crashed. Now just 250 are thought to survive and no-one is sure what happened. The Baw Baw frog lives only in one very small area on a mountain plateau in south-eastern Australia. Its habitat seems to be in good condition and there are no obvious threats to its survival. Whatever caused the catastrophe, it's one of many frog species that's had an unexplained population collapse in recent years.

GREATEST THREAT
DISEASE

MYSTERY LOSS

Around the world, at about the same time of the Baw Baw frog **population crash**, many amphibians disappeared. There are several theories why. Most species that suffered lived at higher altitudes. Could it be something to do with climate change? Maybe levels of air pollution or ultra-violet light became too high? Most scientists now think a frog-killing fungus called chytrid is somehow involved.

HAWKSBILL TURTLE

Beautiful marbled markings on this sea turtle's shell have helped put the species at risk of extinction. Hawksbills are the source of real tortoiseshell, which is now illegal to trade in most countries but has been used extensively worldwide for jewellery and ornaments. These marine turtles feed in ocean waters throughout the tropics, nest on the beaches of many different countries, including Australia, and make long migrations covering thousands of kilometres.

FACT BOX

Multiple challenges

Hawksbills face many threats. Thousands are caught in fishing gear. Their nesting beaches are disturbed. Many die painful deaths after swallowing plastic, and others are struck by boats when they surface to breathe.

LARGETOOTH SAWFISH

This huge sea creature once lived worldwide, but is now extinct in many places, including the United States, though it survives in northern Australia. Sawfish are overfished, since their fins are in high demand for sharkfin soup and their long, tooth-studded snouts are traded by collectors and used in traditional medicines. Even when these fish aren't targets, their snouts often get them caught in lines and nets meant for other species.

HAWAIIAN MONK SEAL

There used to be three monk seal species. The Caribbean monk seal was declared extinct in 1996. The Mediterranean species is on the world's most endangered list (see page 13). And, if the situation doesn't improve for the Hawaiian monk seal, it's likely to be extinct by the middle of this century. There are now only about 600 adults remaining in the wild.

Did you know?

One threat to the Hawaiian monk seal is a lack of food due to overfishing. And it seems that sharks, which have also had their usual food sources depleted by overfishing, are eating more seal pups.

FACT BOX   Hunting victims

Both the Caribbean and Hawaiian monk seals suffered from over-hunting. During the 1800s and 1900s they were slaughtered for their meat, skin and oil made from their blubber, which once had many industrial uses.

◀ DARWIN'S FOX

This fox depends on temperate rainforest for its survival. It was discovered by Charles Darwin in 1834 on Chiloé Island, off the coast of Chile in South America. Today most of the remaining 250 wild individuals of the species survive in a protected national park. But they are threatened by domestic dogs. Dogs will attack these foxes and can also pass diseases onto them.

FACT BOX — **Hopeful searches**

There is a second very small population of Darwin's fox on mainland Chile. It's hoped that by exploring remote pockets of rainforest nearby that other isolated populations of this rare fox species might be found.

CALIFORNIA CONDOR

The California condor is a large type of vulture. It feeds by scavenging on the carcasses of dead animals. Numbers of this bird began falling during the 1800s after many populations of large mammal species that it relied on as a food source were hunted to extinction in its North American home. The condor became protected in 1900, but its numbers continued dropping in large numbers during the 20th century. Scientists eventually identified the cause as lead poisoning from the lead bullets that condors were swallowing when they fed on carcasses left by hunters. The Californian condor was declared extinct in the wild in 1987, when the last eight were taken into a captive breeding program. It was a desperate attempt to save the species but it's been an amazing success. As a result of birds released from the program, there were 104 adults living in the wild by 2012.

GREATEST THREAT

HABITAT LOSS

RED WOLF

Red wolves are a type of wild dog that used to be common in south central and eastern parts of the United States. But their woodland habitat was cleared to make way for agriculture and they were intensely hunted and trapped as pests. When the last 17 wild red wolves were captured in 1980, and taken into a captive breeding program, the species was declared extinct in the wild. Seven years later, red wolves from this program were reintroduced to the wild.

SPECIAL CARE

Hand puppets have been used as substitute parents to help rear chicks in the California condor captive-breeding program.

PROBLEM DOGS

Coyotes are the biggest threat to the reintroduced wolf population. They are a closely related species and inter-breed with the wolves to produce a mixed species.

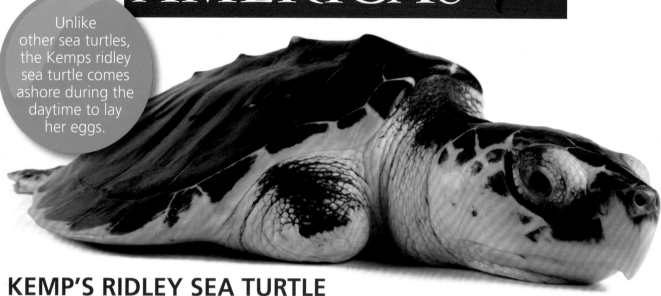

Unlike other sea turtles, the Kemps ridley sea turtle comes ashore during the daytime to lay her eggs.

KEMP'S RIDLEY SEA TURTLE

Kemp's ridley, the most endangered sea turtle species, is found in the Gulf of Mexico and the Atlantic Ocean. In an amazing natural event called an 'arribada', most breeding females emerge from the ocean around the same time each year to nest at just one location – a Mexican beach called Rancho Nuevo. In 1947 more than 40,000 females were filmed doing this. By the 1980s, however, just a few hundred were nesting each year. Too many eggs were being collected by people. And the turtles were being accidentally caught and drowned in prawn trawler nets. Armed guards now protect the nests. And the turtles are kept from trawlers' nets by special 'turtle exclusion devices'. Nesting female numbers are back up to several thousand and the species is very slowly recovering.

GALÁPAGOS PINK LAND IGUANA

This rare pink-and-black-striped lizard was only discovered in 2009 and listed as one of the world's most endangered animals in 2012. There's only one known population and it's extremely small, containing fewer than 200 adults. It lives in dry shrubland on top of an active volcano called Volcan Wolf on the main Galápagos Island, Isabela, in the tropical Pacific Ocean. The volcano has erupted several times during the past century, most recently in 1982.

POSSIBLE PROBLEMS

It's thought that future volcanic eruptions may have a major effect on the species. Black rats and feral cats are also likely to be a threat.

ELEGANT STUBFOOT

Most of world's elegant stubfoot toads used to live in tropical forests in the northwest of the tiny South American country of Ecuador. But that population seems to have disappeared during the past decade. Luckily, there's a small but healthy population surviving on an island called Gorgona, off the coast of Colombia, the South American country just north of Ecuador.

Chytrid fungus can't be ruled out as part of the reason for this disappearance, but usually the disease affects species living higher up in mountains.

LEMUR LEAF FROG

This little amphibian has been hit hard by chytrid – the killer fungus that's been attacking the world's amphibians since the late 1990s. The lemur leaf frog used to be fairly abundant in the tropical forests of Costa Rica and Panama. But most of its natural populations in those two Central American countries have recently either disappeared or massively declined. Habitat degradation may have played a role. But researchers have no doubt the chytrid fungus has been the major cause behind this frog's disappearance.

GREATEST THREAT

DISEASE

FACT BOX — Species safeguard

Since 2001, captive breeding populations of healthy lemur leaf frogs have been kept safe at secure locations in the United States and Britain.

IVORY-BILLED WOODPECKER

GREATEST THREAT

HABITAT LOSS

Huge areas of this woodpecker's forest habitat have been destroyed by logging, mining and agriculture and in 1996 the species was declared extinct. But, in 2004, it was claimed to have been rediscovered in the United States, 60 years after it was last seen there. The rediscovery, however, is controversial. It's based on a few sightings, sound recordings and poor-quality video. There have also been unconfirmed reports the species survives in southern Cuba.

FACT BOX

Hole makers

Ivory-billed woodpeckers need dead and dying trees that they peck at to get at beetle larvae, their main source of food.

PUFFLEGS

These hummingbirds live in specialised forest habitats and woodlands in South America's Andes Mountains. Large areas are being cleared for cattle ranches and crops. And trees are being logged to make charcoal – an important energy source in underdeveloped South America. Education of local communities about how these activities affect pufflegs could help save them.

GREATEST THREAT
HABITAT LOSS

BEING PROTECTED

It is hoped that reserved habitat areas will ensure the future survival of the critically endangered colorful puffleg.

ILLEGAL THREAT

Laws throughout the Americas ban the sale of birds caught in the wild. But, because some collectors pay a lot of money for rare species, there are smugglers who will risk fines and prison sentences to illegally catch and trade birds. Studies show that many tens of thousands of wild-caught birds are traded illegally every year around the world.

BLOND CAPUCHIN

There are fewer than 200 adult individuals of this small South American monkey still alive in the wild. They're spread between 24 separate populations along the coast, none of which are in protected areas. The reason so few survive is because much of the blond capuchin's coastal forest home in northeast Brazil has been destroyed, mostly to make way for sugarcane farms. It is also hunted for food, and it's babies are taken away as pets.

POORLY KNOWN

By the time the blond capuchin was properly described by science, in 2006, it had already become one of the world's rarest primates.

PYGMY RACCOON

Some of the main threats to pygmy raccoons come from introduced animals. The raccoons live only on Cozumel Island, off Mexico's coast, where they forage mostly for crabs and crayfish. Domestic dogs and cats attack them, compete for their food and can infect them with diseases and parasites. Pressure from the tourist industry is also being felt by pygmy raccoons. This is expanding in coastal areas of Cozumel Island where the raccoons prefer to live.

DISASTER THREAT

The pygmy raccoon population on Cozumel Island is now so small that scientists believe the whole species could be wiped out by just one hurricane.

MACAWS

Macaws are parrots from South and Central America. Many have beautiful feathers, which has made them popular as pets and with bird enthusiasts. Sadly, overcollecting has caused population crashes in many species. Bolivia's blue-throated macaw has suffered severely from this threat. It was thought to be extinct in the wild but a small number were rediscovered in 1992. It remains extremely rare, which makes it even more prized by collectors.

STILL MISSING

The glaucous macaw hasn't been seen in the wild since the 1960s but experts hope it survives in a remote location not yet found by collectors.

WHAT CAN WE DO?

RESCUING HABITAT

The number one threat to the world's endangered animals is habitat loss and degradation. That includes the destruction of natural forests by logging for timber or clearing to make way for crops. And it includes polluting the oceans with rubbish; draining the water out of wetlands; and changing the types of plants growing on grasslands.

Even the busiest city landscapes can be habitat for native animals, if they're looked after. For example, New York, the city with the biggest area in the world, is becoming cleaner and greener. Some animals that once lived there but hadn't been seen for a long time have been returning. These include white-tailed deer, wild turkeys, harbour seals and peregrine falcons.

Did you know?

Sydney is Australia's biggest city, and even there you're able to find beautiful birds, possums, bandicoots, gliders, lizards, snakes, frogs and lots of insects!

YOUR PATCH

If you have a backyard, you can turn it into you own little piece of 'natural habitat', by planting the sorts of plants that would have once grown in your area. Get ideas about what to plant from your local council or bush regeneration group. Your backyard could become a little oasis for local native birds, butterflies and perhaps even small mammals, frogs and lizards.

Don't forget, wherever possible, to re-use and recycle any materials you use. This helps to lower pollution and reduce the pressure to produce new materials, which is always a good thing for natural habitats.

BUY SMART

Take an interest in what you eat and use and where it comes from. For example, many of the processed foods we eat, including biscuits, contain palm oil. Huge areas of tropical rainforests are now being logged for this oil. After habitat loss, illegal hunting is the next biggest threat to many of the world's animals. Make sure you don't buy products that come from endangered animals. This is not likely to be an issue in Australia, because of the laws that have been designed to prevent it. But you might come across banned animal products while on holidays, in places such as Indonesia, China or Mexico. Sometimes you'll even see live animals, such as sea turtle babies, for sale in market places.

GET RESPONSIBLE

We use a lot of products from forests, from toilet paper to wood. You can make sure the things you use have come from a sustainable source. That might be a plantation specially planted, which means that a natural forest hasn't been knocked down.

One way to tell if the products you use come from a sustainable source is to see if they have a stamp from the Forestry Stewardship Council (FSC). This is an international not-for-profit organisation trying to make sure that the world's forests are managed responsibly.

GET INVOLVED

Support national parks and wildlife sanctuaries. These are places where you'll find natural habitats and endangered animals that are being protected. You could volunteer to help out, or just visit.

Zoos are another place where you may be able to volunteer to help animals. Modern zoos are so much more than just places to see animals. Many now also run conservation programs, or have captive breeding programs for rare and endangered species. Some will have programs where you or your school can get involved by 'adopting' endangered animals.

Glossary

black market	Illegal buying and selling of a rare item.
captive breeding	The controlled breeding of animals away from their natural environments, usually in zoos or sanctuaries.
Chinese medicine	A traditional medicine system, originally from China but now practised throughout Asia and other parts of the world; it uses herbs, minerals, and animal products as well as acupuncture, massage, and exercise.
deforestation	The process of clearing natural forest, often by logging or burning.
extinction	The death of a species.
habitat	The natural home of a species.
overexploitation	The use of a natural resource, such as a population of fish or a herd of antelope, at a rate that can't be sustained or continued.
poaching	Illegally hunting, trapping or killing animals.
primates	The animal group that includes human, apes and monkeys.
population crash	A sudden fall in the total number of individuals in an animal group.

FURTHER READING

The Atlas of Endangered Animals
Paula Hammond
2010, Cavendish Square Publishing

Survival
Stanley Johnson & Robert Vagg
2010, Interlink Pub Group

John Gould's Extinct and Endangered Mammals
Fred Ford
2014, National Library of Australia

Vanishing Act
2005, Art Wolfe